TURNING YOUR FROWN UPSIDE DOWN

POETRY AND SCRIPTURE

SHARON MOORE

Scripture quotations are from the New International Version (NIV). Copyright © 1973, 1978, 1984, 2011 by Biblica, Inc. Used by permission. All rights reserved worldwide.

Turning Your Frown Upside Down
Copyright © 2024 by Sharon Moore

All rights reserved. No part of this publication may be reproduced, distributed, or transmitted in any form or by any means, including photocopying, recording, or other electronic or mechanical methods, without the prior written permission of the author, except in the case of brief quotations embodied in critical reviews and certain other non-commercial uses permitted by copyright law.

Tellwell Talent
www.tellwell.ca

ISBN
978-1-77962-188-7 (Hardcover)
978-1-77962-056-9 (Paperback)
978-1-77962-057-6 (eBook)

PREFACE

Throughout the years I have enjoyed writing poetry. They are very unique in that some tell a story, some will give you hope in the midst of despair, while others will warm your heart. Each poem is also accompanied by a scripture verse for additional reflection.

My biggest intent is that by reading these poems you will find inspiration and enjoyment, as well as pull up some fond memories of your own. Plus, there are some that are truly created to help - turn your frown upside down!

Note: I am donating 25% of all proceeds from the sale of my book to ServeUkraine. Their relational connections allow them to address physical, mental, spiritual, and practical needs.

Sharon Moore

TABLE OF CONTENTS

Preface iii
Being a Mother Means 1
When I Thought You Were Not Looking............ 3
I Know an Old Lady 5
Taken Back in Time... 7
The Fix-it Man.. 9
Father's Day Dilemma..11
Thank You Mom 12
Outlook 13
God Knows What to Do.....................................14
Attitude Check..15
My Favorite Picnic Place....................................16
Being a Teacher Means.......................................18
Memorial Day A Day to Remember 20
I Wish I Could Have Been There 22
Perspective On Christian Growth 24
Giver of Love... 26
What a Genius!..28
The Pearl.. 30
You Brightened Up Our Life 31
My Special Friend 33

The Time Has Come	35
Giving All I've Got	36
If You Could Be Anything	37
Labor of Love	38
Keep In Touch!	40
Other books by Sharon Moore	41
About the Author	46

BEING A MOTHER MEANS

Being a mother means
   never taking a bath alone,
      jellybeans and ice cream cones.

Getting up at half-past three,
   peaking around corners where
      mischief might be.

Little hurts, great big tears,
   animal noises for big cheers.

Little toes, another spill,
   first time words, oh what a thrill.

Being a mother means coloring books
   and ABCs, lots of toys,
      "May I have that please."

Story time now off to bed,
   "But sissy hit me on my head."

A rocking chair, with that special squeak,
   cuddle blanket for good sleep.

Day is done, but you're not through.
   now there are those dishes to do.

Sharon Moore

Being a mother means
   sometimes feeling weary,
      sometimes feeling drained,
         sometimes you may feel as if
            you might just go insane.

But that little one is growing,
   and changing every day,
      from that little babe inside you,
         to a person, come what may.

Children are so special,
   a gift from God above.
      They will fill your house with happiness
         and fill your heart with love.

She is clothed with strength and dignity; she can laugh at the days to come. She speaks with wisdom, and faithful instruction is on her tongue. She watches over the affairs of her household and does not eat the bread of idleness.

                                              Proverbs 31:25-27

WHEN I THOUGHT YOU WERE NOT LOOKING

When I thought you were not looking,
I laughed when you were 2,
Dancing round and round till you
almost had to spew.

When I thought you were not looking,
I would actually take a peek,
To make sure that you were safe
when playing hide and seek.

When I thought you were not looking,
I remember being proud,
When you walked across the stage,
in your cap and gown.

When I thought you were not looking
my heart was filled with joy,
When you told me you wanted to marry,
such a wonderful, loving boy.

When I thought you were not looking,
tears come from my eyes
When I think about my special girl
and how time really flies.

Sharon Moore

The time we had together
seems brief when you compare,
but knowing that you are in good hands

makes it something I can bare.
When I thought you were not looking…

I LOOKED

And wanted to say THANKS sweet daughter of mine,
for all the things I saw…
when you thought I was not looking,
and that's the best of all

That person is like a tree planted by streams of water, which yields its fruit in season and whose leaf does not wither whatever they do prospers.
Psalm 1:3

I KNOW AN OLD LADY

I know an old lady who had a big cry.
I don't know why she had such a cry.
Perhaps she'll die.

I know an old lady who had a big cry due to
the problems she held deep inside.
She swallowed her problems which made her cry.
But I don't know why she had such a cry. Perhaps
she'll die.

I know an old lady who became quite distraught.
Oh, my how she fought,
to not be distraught.
She became distraught, in the midst of a big cry,
due to the problems she held deep inside.
She swallowed her problems which made her cry.
But I don't know why she had such a cry. Perhaps
she'll die.

I know an old lady who prayed to the Lord,
a confession of fault that He was ignored.
But she prayed to the Lord about being distraught and
oh how she fought
from being distraught.

She became distraught, in midst of a big cry, due to the problems she held deep inside. She swallowed her problems which made her cry. But this time she said,

"I don't want to cry!"

Soooo, I know an old lady who started spending time in God's word, a friendship was learned by spending time in God's word.

She read God's word to know more about Him, a trust was formed and then to begin…in knowing more about Him, she learned to love God greater, a promise she made not to give up later.
There was an old lady with worries no more, because she soon learned to <u>rest</u> in the Lord. When she learned to rest in the Lord, she had worries no more.

So, the next time she cries,
she knows now she won't die!

Even to your old age and gray hairs I am He; I am He who will sustain you. I have made you and I will carry you; I will sustain you and I will rescue you.

Isaiah 46:4

TAKEN BACK IN TIME

I remember when I was young
    The thing I'd like to do
Was to visit my Grandma and Grandpa
    And spend a week or two.

Whenever I hear a whippoorwill sing
    Or see clothes hanging from a line,
See bacon sizzling in an iron pan,
    I am taken back in time.

To when Grandma would make her grape jelly
    By running it through a stocking sieve,
And I would spend a whole day shopping,
    With the little money she'd give.
They lived in a very small town
    Where we could find treasures galore,
By running down the aisles
    At the Five and Ten Cent store.

My Grandpa always worked hard to provide,
    But he would take time to play.
He would bounce us on both knees
    And take walks in the mid of day.

Now they live up in heaven,
    They've been gone for many a year.
But I don't have to worry
    Or shed even one tear.

Sharon Moore

For whenever I hear a whippoorwill sing
    Or see clothes hanging on a line,
See bacon sizzling in an iron pan,
    I am taken back in time.

Be devoted to one another in love. Honor one another above yourselves.
Romans 12:10

THE FIX-IT MAN

(dedicated to My Dad)

If there's a squeak in the gate,
If there's a crack in the road,
If there's a frame to be hung,
He can get it done!

If there is a fish to be had,
If there is a joke to be told,
We know in a heartbeat
He will make it good as gold!

This man of which I talk of
Lived an incredibly full life,
With his adoring family
and his precious, faithful wife.

He's been a faithful servant,
With service to our land,
A Lt. Colonel in the Army
Was his high command.

An administrator to the children
of Central Junior High.
A carpenter of homes,
He crafted on the side.

Sharon Moore

He touched the lives of many
With his humor and his love,
By giving unto others his gifts from above.
A "Fix-it" man we called him
Because he could do it all.
From broken hearts and shattered dreams,
To plaster on the wall.

They tell us that Heaven is perfect,
And we believe that to be true,
But surely God in heaven,
He could fix a thing or two.
So, make a list of jobs,
For he has so much to share,
He can fix anything You want,
Even way up there!

I thank my God every time I remember you.

Philippians 1:3

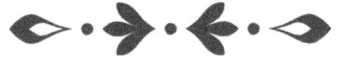

FATHER'S DAY DILEMMA

Each of us would just like to say,
We love you in so many ways.
But getting you something is getting quite hard,
And besides, you said, "Just give me a card."

However, I wanted to give you a whole lot more,
Something terrific you find from a store.
But the car went on the fritz,
The bills were compounding,
Our rent cost a lot; life seems so confounding.

So, I hope you enjoy the gift I've enclosed
It is not something fancy,
Tied with ribbons and bows.
It has even been recycled,
Because it came from you to me.
It is the gift of love, for all the world to see.

My command is this: Love each other as I have loved you.
                                                John 15:12

THANK YOU MOM

Thanks for all the wonderful things you do
That make my life complete.
With a helping hand, a loving heart
And wonderful, sweet treats.

Thank you for letting Jesus shine
Through all that you do.
From teaching kids to cleaning house,
There's nothing you two can't muddle through.

But most of all I just want to say,
That I love you in every way.
You have showered me with love
Beyond what could be measured.
Thank you, Mom for giving me
A life of endless pleasure.

*Her children arise and call her blessed; her husband also, and he praises her:
"Many women do noble things, but you surpass them all."*

Proverbs 31:28–29

OUTLOOK

They say a smile is a frown turned
Upside down, and I know this to be true.
For many times I have experienced this Flip-flop
thanks to thoughts of you.

You have a way of making
The gray clouds disappear,
By sharing a positive outlook
That makes one want to cheer.

So when life gets overwhelming
And problems begin to compound,
I hope to share this lesson
That your frown is upside down.

A friend loves at all times, and a brother is born for a time of adversity.
Proverbs 17:17

GOD KNOWS WHAT TO DO

When life's constant struggles
Seem to get you down,
Your feet can't find the solid ground,
There is not a shred of happiness
To be found,
God knows what to do.

When your will power shows its might,
To determine who will win the fight,
All cry of a broken heart by night,
God knows what to do.

When you decide to surrender all,
To give to Him, so you won't fall,
To be a servant, to answer the call,
God knows what to do.

He will give you strength
To see you through,
He will send His Spirit to comfort you,
Just believe that His love is true,
God knows what to do...
He will take care of You!

So do not fear, for I am with you; do not be dismayed, for I am your God. I will strengthen you and help you; I will uphold you with my righteous right hand.

Isaiah 42:10

ATTITUDE CHECK

A bear climbed up a big, tall tree.
He found a hive with lots of bees.
The bees got mad, the bear climbed fast,
Bee stings sure can really last.

The moral of this story is plain to see,
That ups and downs are bound to be.
God takes care of each of us,
But now and then we might get stuck.

To spread love and laughter is the key
And the attitude of what is to be.
For contentment is what dwells inside,
Even on a bumpy ride.

So even if you're in a slump,
Remember please don't be a grump.
To all around you must be fair,
Or you might turn into a bear!

Peace I leave with you; my peace I give you. I do not give to you as the world gives. Do not let your hearts be troubled and do not be afraid.
John14:27

MY FAVORITE PICNIC PLACE

My favorite picnic place is full of
Great surprises,
With a spring fed waterfall
And a raspberry patch beside us.

This place has so much beauty
It's a wonder to behold,
With birds a singing
Seashells ringing
And flowers bright and bold.

There're never any pesky pests
Who sneak up with a sting,
Or poison oak and ivy
To ruin my big fling.
And if I ever get the urge
To take a great big hike,
There are a lot of nice clean bathrooms
So I can make my hike alright.

I'm so glad I have this special place
In which I can unwind,
To have that worthwhile luxury
Of wasting lots of time.

Turning Your Frown Upside Down

So, when things get rushed and ragged
All done with lots of haste.
I pack up my bags,
Run out of the door,
To my favorite picnic place.

You will go out in joy and be led forth in peace; the mountains and hills will burst into song before you, and all the trees of the field will clap their hands.
                                                                Isaiah 55:12

BEING A TEACHER MEANS

Being a teacher means lesson plans and ABCs
    Having patience for all of these.
Storytime and Show & Tell;
    Mickey quit pulling that little girl's hair.
Never having enough time alone;
    Announcements needing a megaphone.
Little hurts, great big tears;
    Recess time brings lots of cheers.

Being a teacher means looking forward to half-
    past three.
Peeking around corners where
    Mischief might be.
Getting kids dressed to go out in the cold;
    Reminders to empty their cubbyholes.
A full day spent with little ones in your care;
    Now your family needs time to spare.
Day is done, but you're not through,
    Now there are those lesson plans to do.

Being a teacher means sometimes you may feel
    Weary, sometimes you feel drained,
Sometimes you may feel as if you might just go
    Insane.

But these little ones are growing,
    They are changing every day,
And we can all be proud of the progress
    They have made.
For you've taught them the
    Importance of sharing;
You taught them their ABCs,
    You taught them how to write their names.

More important than all of these,
    Is that you never gave up for a minute,
You knew the potential they had,
    You taught them their lessons without delay,
Even when they were bad.
    So, even if we don't say it, as often as we should
Thank you for being the kind of teacher
    That far surpasses good!

Start children off on the way they should go, and even when they are old they will not turn from it.

Proverbs 22:6

MEMORIAL DAY A DAY TO REMEMBER

Memorial Day is here
So what first comes to mind?
My bank is closed, a day off work
And mail will be behind.

Here in Indiana we cherish our 500 race
And have hopes that this year's winner
Will have a female face.

At church things go as usual
Not much difference from the rest,
Except for a message to the children
That soldiers gave their best.
I then head towards the cemetery
Where my parents now rest in peace.
My heart is touched as I reach the entrance
Full size flags adorn the streets.

People gather round their loved ones.
Their hearts are empty still,
With a longing to be with that name
That a rock in their place can't fill.

At a cemetery called Arlington,
The head stones multiply.
For conflict continues to rob our land
Of young men and women who have died.

History seems to repeat itself
Time and time again.
As war continues to take the lives
For freedom we hope to win.

Memorial Day is here and let us not forget,
That this day was made especially
To remember the service of our Vets.

Protecting us from harm
Is what was meant to be.
We might not agree with the leaders,
But I hope that all will see....
That Memorial Day is here for a reason,
Sacrifice has been made for you and me.
All with hopes of making
America, The Land of the Free.

Greater love has no one than this: to lay down one's life for one's friends.
John 15:13

I WISH I COULD HAVE BEEN THERE

I wish I could have been there
That first Christmas Day,
So that I could have seen the
Angels in all of Their array.
I would have joined in singing
As the angels sang That day,
Praise to God almighty
For our King is born today.

I wish I could have been there
That first Christmas day,
So that I could have seen
The precious babe in a stable lay.
I would have bowed in reverence
And from my heart would say,
Praise to God almighty
For our King is born today.

I wished I could have been there
That first Christmas day,
I would make Him a beautiful card
And in the middle say…
I love you dear, sweet Jesus
For all you have done for me,

You have made it so my life is good
For all eternity.
And thank you for your sweet, sweet spirit
Of which has had a part
Of showing me the way to live
Of which I'll not depart.

So Praise to you sweet Jesus,
You have shown me the way
And praise to God almighty...
For our King is born today.

*For to us a child is born, to us a son is given,
and the government will be on his shoulders.
And he will be called Wonderful Counselor, Mighty God,
Everlasting Father, Prince of Peace.*

Isaiah 9:6

PERSPECTIVE ON CHRISTIAN GROWTH

Going off to church can often be a drag,
you have to dress up nice with pantyhose that sag.

My Mom said I must go to learn about this man who died upon a cross with nails dug in his hands.

To me it sounds so scary, I think I'll wait a while and scurry off to play, for I'm just a little child.

I'm growing more, my life is full, a boy just looked my way. My heart beats fast, my hands go cold, I'm not sure what to say.

The time I have is limited, church must wait again, because I want to show my peers that I am one of them.

Well now I'm all grown up, with children of my own and struggling every day to make my house a home.
I ask the Lord to guide me in every step I take, so that the things I say and do won't be a big mistake.
Church has become more vital; I finally understand the sacrifice God made for every living man.

He knows we can't be perfect. He knows we'll miss
the mark. All He asks in return is to open up our heart. Then we will get to see all the treasures He has in store, with blessings beyond belief and the key to heaven's door.

And now I sometimes smile when I hear my daughter
say, "Mom, do we really have to go to church again
today? For going off to church can often be a drag,
you have to dress up nice with pantihose that sag.

Therefore let us move beyond the elementary teachings about Christ and be taken forward to maturity.

Hebrews 6:1(a)

GIVER OF LOVE

Giver of Love, Giver of Love
Please help me to be a giver of love.
Sending down your strength from above
To help me be a giver of love.

I want to be a giver of love,
He's forgiven me so many times.
For if it weren't for the cross
How might I survive?

My sins would be the death of me,
And where might I find hope?
This world is full of so much pain,
No wonder some can't cope.
Giver of Love, Giver of Love
Please help me to be a giver of love.
Sending down your strength from above
To help me be a giver of love.

His love gives my life purpose,
There's a message to all friends,
That freedom might be yours,
But Heaven's not the end.

You search for joy in other ways,
And though I do not boast,
I hope you see from deep in me
God's Love is what you need most.

Giver of Love, Giver of Love
Please help me to be a giver of love.
Sending down your strength from above
To help me be a giver of love.

Love is patient, love is kind. It does not envy, it does not boast, it is not proud. It does not dishonor others, it is not self-seeking, it is not easily angered, it keeps no record of wrongs. Love does not delight in evil but rejoices with the truth. It always protects, always trusts, always hopes, always perseveres.

1 Corinthians 13:4-7

WHAT A GENIUS!

God wrote out the songs for
The robin to sing.
He made the beautiful trees
Which bloom in the Spring.

He made us all different
So that we could all see
The uniqueness of His love
For everything.

What a God, full of love!
What a God, so divine!
That He came to earth
For this sin of mine.

He even gives us precious friends
On whom we can rely.
But thank you most of all
For being by my side.

Sometimes the road gets rocky.
Sometimes it is hard to bear.
But I know that you are with me,
In a whisper of a prayer.

Turning Your Frown Upside Down

You have been given the nickname Helper,
And I know that to be true,
Because of all of the struggles,
You were there to help me through.

I look to You with eyes of faith through
Circumstances I cannot understand.
But I know without a doubt
That you are there to hold my hand.

I love you God with all my heart
And I hope that it is plain to see,
That you are always there for us,
For all eternity.

Oh, the depth of the riches of the wisdom and knowledge of God! How unsearchable his judgments, and his paths beyond tracing out!
Romans 11:33

THE PEARL

Dedicated to my sister

The pearl is something precious
    When you think of its origin,
Of how an oyster worked so hard
    This really was an obsession to him.

He wanted to make something pretty,
    But all he could find was a rock,
So, he scraped, and he scrubbed,
    And he scrubbed and he scraped,
Till that rock was out of his knocks.

Now that you are ready to be out on your own
    I just had to let you know,
That even though you are my sister,
    I do love you so.

So, I asked my little oyster friend,
    "Would you please give up your pearl?
So that my twin sister will always see,
    That she is so very precious to me!"

She is more precious than rubies; nothing you desire compare with her.
                                                            Proverbs 3:15

YOU BRIGHTENED UP OUR LIFE

Memorial to my nephew

There once was a boy who came into our lives.
His heart was as good as gold.
At times he was quite impish,
But he mostly did what told.

He made us laugh, he made us smile,
By the things he would say
By the things he would do.
Little dear one, we will always love you!

He went to go to heaven,
With all the loved ones there,
And of course to see our Savior
Who has him in his loving care.
We know that he is in good hands.
We know that he is having fun,
But sometimes we miss him so very much,
This precious dear loved one.

Sometimes it will be hard
To go on without this little child,
But we will do our best
By remembering his smile.

Sharon Moore

Our lives will keep on going
Amidst our toil and strife,
But we will remember this sweet little boy
Who brightened up our life.

Blessed are those who mourn, for they will be comforted.
                                                              Matthew 5:4

MY SPECIAL FRIEND

I have a special friend
Who means so much to me
His love has changed my life,
So now I live abundantly.

Sure, sometimes I get discouraged,
Especially with the way things are today,
But it is so very nice to know
That He will guide my way.

I love Him so very much
Because He really cares
And because he has the answer
To my every prayer.
Sometimes it may be yes,
Sometimes it may be no.
Sometimes it may be wait,
Because He loves us so.

Jesus is that precious one
Of whom I speak about,
Who cared enough to die for me
So that sin I'd be without.

Sharon Moore

And now I hope that all can see
Just what my Jesus means to me
And if you came to ask him in,
I know He'd be your lifelong friend.

One who has unreliable friends soon comes to ruin, but there is a friend who sticks closer than a brother.
                                                            Proverbs 18:24

THE TIME HAS COME

Father God who reigns on high
Peering in solace through the sky,
Is your heart breaking from what you see?
Is there anything left that was meant to be?

We fear the dangers of the night
And are consumed with pressures of everyday life
Where all the good morals seem to be breaking.
Father God, Your heart must be aching.

For the reason you made us was for fellowship sweet.
To sing songs of praise, to grow complete.
You even gave us Your Word as our guide,
But some want to change it for their sins to justify.
So, Father, I ask in humbleness please,
That You would look farther than all of these.
For deep inside a little heart,
You once heard us say we would do our part.

To shine our light 'till Jesus comes.
And Father, we know there's lots of work to get done.
The Time has come to do our part,
To shout, "I Love You!" with all my heart!

He has shown you, O mortal, what is good.
And what does the L ORD *require of you?*
To act justly and to love mercy and to walk humbly with your God.
                                                            Micah 6:8

GIVING ALL I'VE GOT

I may not be an Olympian
I may not be a star,
But I think that it is important
To be the best you are.

As a student one must study hard
In order to make the grade.
As an artist it takes patience
With all that's to be made.

Practice and endurance
Can often be the key,
With a little bit of talent
And ingenuity.
Mistakes can even play a part
In the growth that's to take place,
Because it's part of a process
Which brings maturity and grace.

So even if the record books
Don't list me at the top,
I know that I've done my best
By giving all I've got.

For we are God's handiwork, created in Christ Jesus to do good works, which God prepared in advance for us to do.

Ephesians 2:10

IF YOU COULD BE ANYTHING

If you could be anything, what would you be?
If I was a bird, I would soar across the sky and land on a branch looking down from on high.

If I was an otter, it would be lots of fun, to swim down the river until the day was done.

If I was a pig, I could play and get muddy, all day long with my good buddy.

If I was a fish, I would swim in the sea, deep inside the ocean is where I want to be.

God made me special there is no one else like me, and I get to explore all that I want to be.

If I was an athlete, I could run in a race, I could score a soccer goal or dance with pure grace.

If I was a mechanic, I could repair a car. Or if I was a pilot, I could travel really far.

If I could be anything, what would I be?
The answer is easy, I want to be ME!

*For I know the plans I have for you, declares the L*ORD*, plans to prosper you and not to harm you, plans to give you hope and a future.*
                                                            Jeremiah 29:11

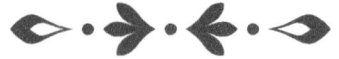

LABOR OF LOVE

Dedicated to senior care providers

I wake them up, I get them dressed,
I brush their hair, so they look their best.
I make their bed and wash their clothes,
The little things that no one knows.

I hold their hand when they are scared,
And talk to them when no one's there.
My goal is simple as I strive above
To leave them with no doubt that…
They Are Loved!

Dear children, let us not love with words or speech but with actions and in truth.

1 John 3:18

ACKNOWLEDGMENTS

I wish to thank my husband, Greg Moore. As a writer and editor for over 25 years at Indiana University, I definitely appreciate him providing a professional critique.

KEEP IN TOUCH!

My author website:
https://www.sharonmoorefun.org/

OTHER BOOKS BY SHARON MOORE

IF YOU COULD BE ANYTHING

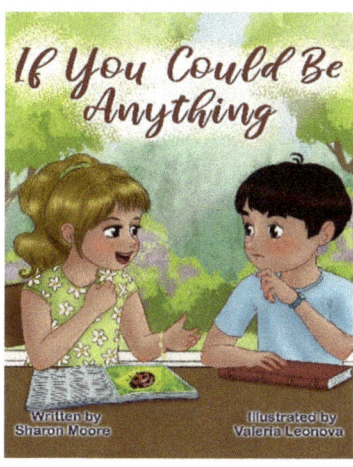

If You Could Be Anything encourages children to explore their imagination and think about what they would like to be if they could be anything. The book features rhyming verses that describe different animals and professions, such as birds, otters, pigs, athletes, mechanics, and pilots. This book has beautiful illustrations, and the plot of the story is to encourage kids to be the best that they can be and impact the world with their special abilities.

THAT FIRST CHRISTMAS DAY

Come join a little girl on her journey to the first Christmas, where she sees baby Jesus and the angels. She loves it so much that she draws baby Jesus a beautiful card to express her love. This story helps to make Christmas a more personal experience, with illustrations that will capture your heart and activity pages at the end.

THE FROG POND

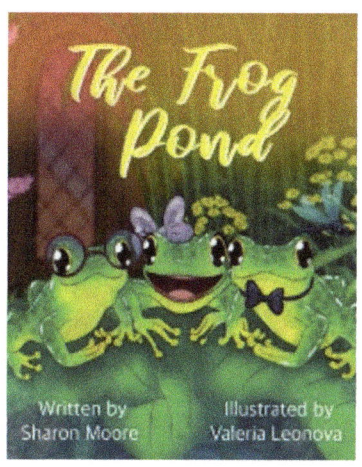

Join Herbie, Fergie, and Gerdie as they become young frogs, and help children learn invaluable life lessons. Plus, this is a fun, interactive book. Your kids will love doing the Froggy Hoedown & a special - Froggy Cheer!

THE SPARROW FAMILY

Meet the Sparrow family. Watch them grow up and arrive at the most important moment of their life: learning to fly. Facing their fears, the chicks leave the nest on a wing and a prayer and imitate Mom and Dad.

Turning Your Frown Upside Down

LINDA THE LADYBUG GOES TO HEAVEN

By: Miss Sharon

Come take a tour of Heaven through the eyes of an inquisitive ladybug name Linda, in my book entitled - Linda the Ladybug Goes To Heaven. If you have a little one who is having a hard time dealing with the loss of a loved one, this could help.

ABOUT THE AUTHOR

Sharon Moore loves to share the gospel message through creative arts. Writing poetry, books for children, painting nature and playing her violin/fiddle in a bluegrass band and for local senior care facilities have all become an outreach ministry for her. To see examples, check out her website:

sharonmoorefun.org

www.ingramcontent.com/pod-product-compliance
Lightning Source LLC
LaVergne TN
LVHW072023060526
838200LV00058B/4659